Competitive Dance

by Julie Murray

Abdo Kids Jumbo is an Imprint of Abdo Kids
abdobooks.com

abdobooks.com

Published by Abdo Kids, a division of ABDO, P.O. Box 398166, Minneapolis, Minnesota 55439. Copyright © 2023 by Abdo Consulting Group, Inc. International copyrights reserved in all countries. No part of this book may be reproduced in any form without written permission from the publisher. Abdo Kids Jumbo™ is a trademark and logo of Abdo Kids.

Printed in the United States of America, North Mankato, Minnesota.

102022
012023

Photo Credits: AP Images, Getty Images, Shutterstock

Production Contributors: Teddy Borth, Jennie Forsberg, Grace Hansen
Design Contributors: Candice Keimig, Pakou Moua

Library of Congress Control Number: 2022937168
Publisher's Cataloging-in-Publication Data

Names: Murray, Julie, author.
Title: Competitive dance / by Julie Murray
Description: Minneapolis, Minnesota : Abdo Kids, 2023 | Series: Artistic sports | Includes online resources and index.
Identifiers: ISBN 9781098264215 (lib. bdg.) | ISBN 9781098264772 (ebook) | ISBN 9781098265052 (Read-to-Me ebook)
Subjects: LCSH: Dance--Juvenile literature. | Dance--Competitions--Juvenile literature. | Dance teams--Juvenile literature. | Sports--Juvenile literature. | Sports--History--Juvenile literature.
Classification: DDC 792.8--dc23

Table of Contents

Competitive Dance 4	More Facts 22
History 10	Glossary 23
Skills 16	Index 24
Teams 18	Abdo Kids Code 24

Competitive Dance

Competitive dance is a popular sport. Dancers compete in different types of dance. Jazz, hip-hop, and ballet are just a few common styles.

Dancers are judged in competitions. Judges award points for different parts of each dance, like **technique** and **choreography**. The dancer with the highest total points is the winner.

Dancers are grouped by their age and skill level. They compete in different sized teams or on their own. Most dance **routines** are performed with music.

History

People have been dancing for thousands of years. Carvings and paintings in ancient Egyptian tombs and caves show people dancing 10,000 years ago.

Competitive dance became popular in the early 1900s. Dance halls opened for competitions. People also participated in **dance marathons**.

The first dance studios opened in the 1930s. Many more opened their doors in the 1960s and 1970s. These training centers pushed **competitive** dance to a new level.

Skills

Dancing is physically demanding. Dancers must be strong and healthy. They need to be **flexible** and have good balance.

17

Teams

Dance centers usually have **competitive** teams. Many dancers compete for their school. Tryouts are held each year for dancers to earn a spot on the team.

Dancers have different teams to choose from. Jazz, hip-hop, high kick, and **pom dance** are all popular. The teams often perform at school sporting events. They also compete in local and national events.

21

More Facts

- The first World Dance Championship was held in Paris, France, in 1909.

- Reality TV shows like *So You Think You Can Dance* and *World of Dance* have renewed an interest in **competitive** dance.

- The Dance Worlds competition is held at Walt Disney World in Orlando, Florida. Dancers from around the world compete for the title of "World Champion."

Glossary

choreography – the art of planning and performing the sequence of steps and movements in dance.

competitive – having to do with or decided by competition.

dance marathon – an event in which people dance or walk to music for an extended period of time. Can be competitive or for enjoyment.

flexible – easily bent without breaking.

pom dance – dancing while using pom poms that is mainly performed by high school and college students during halftime at sporting events.

routine – a worked-out part that may be often repeated.

technique – the particular method or way of doing or performing something.

Index

ancient Egypt 10

ballet 4

competition 6, 8, 12, 14, 18, 20

dance hall 12

dance marathon 12

dance studios 14, 18

dancers 4, 6, 8, 16, 18, 20

high kick 20

hip-hop 4, 20

history 10, 12, 14

jazz 4, 20

judging 6

music 8

physical health 16

pom dance 20

routine 8

teams 8, 18, 20

tryouts 18

Visit **abdokids.com** to access crafts, games, videos, and more!

Use Abdo Kids code **ACK4215** or scan this QR code!